S

MW01274359

-1995

F-3908
x5

GARY GEDDES
Active Trading

Selected Poems, 1970-1995

PETERLOO POETS

First published in the U.K. in 1996 by Peterloo Poets
2 Kelly Gardens, Calstock, Cornwall PL18 9SA, U.K.

Co-published by Peterloo Poets and Goose Lane Editions, Canada,
1996.

Cover illustration: "Rebuilding a caravel" by Theodore de Bry, 1594.
Edited by Laurel Boone.
Book design by Julie Scriver, Goose Lane Editions.
Printed in Canada by Hignell Printing.

A cataloguing record for this book is available
from the British Library.

ISBN 1-871471-51-6

CONTENTS

BOOKS by GARY GEDDES

ACKNOWLEDGEMENTS

for Duck, Beam, Juniper and Sam

Poetry is mortal breath that knows it's mortal.
— *Robert Hass*

*To whisper for that which has been lost. Not out of
nostalgia, but because it is on the site of loss that hopes
are born.*
— *John Berger*

*In the broken thing, moreover, human agency is oddly
implied; breakage, whatever its cause, is the dark
complement to the act of making . . .*
— *Louise Glück*

LETTER OF THE MASTER OF HORSE (1973)*

I was signed
on the King's authority
as master of horse.
Three days
          (I remember
          quite clearly)
three days after we parted.
I did not really believe it,
it seemed so much the unrolling
of an incredible dream.

＊

Bright plumes, scarlet tunics,
glint of sunlight on armour.
Fifty of the King's best horses,
strong, high-spirited, rearing
to the blast of trumpets,
galloping
down the long avenida
to the waiting ships.
And me, your gangling brother,
permitted to ride with cavalry.

＊

Laughter,
children singing
in the market, women
dancing, throwing flowers,
the whole street covered
with flowers.

---

*This poem was composed in 1970, when it won the E.J. Pratt Prize.
It was first published in 1973.

In the Plaza del Sol
a blind beggar kissed my eyes.
I hadn't expected the softness
of his fingers
                moving upon my face.

             *

A bad beginning.
The animals knew, hesitated
at the ramps, backed off,
finally had to be blindfolded
and beaten aboard.

Sailors grumbled for days
as if we had brought on board
a cargo of women.

             *

But the sea smiled.
Smiled as we passed
through the world's gate,
smiled as we lost our escort
of gulls. I have seen
such smiles on faces of whores
in Barcelona.

             *

For months now
an unwelcome guest
in my own body.
I squat by the fire
in a silence broken only
by the tireless grinding
of insects.

I have taken
to drawing your face

in the brown earth
at my feet
        (The ears are
        never quite right.)

    *

You are waving,
waving. Your
tears are a river
that swells, rushes beside me.

I lie for days
in a sea drier than the desert
of the Moors
but your tears are lost,
sucked
into the parched throat of the sky.

    *

I am watched daily.
The ship's carpenter is at work
nearby, within the stockade,
fashioning a harness for me,
a wooden collar. He is a fool
who takes no pride in his work,
yet the chips lie about his feet
beautiful as yellow petals.

    *

Days melt
in the hot sun, flow
together. An order is given
to jettison the horses,
it sweeps like a breeze
over parched black faces.

    *

I am not consulted, though
Ortega comes to me later
when it is over and says:

> God knows, there are men
> I'd have worried less to lose.

    *

The sailors are relieved,
fall to it with abandon.
The first horse is blindfolded,
led to the gunwales, and struck
so hard it leaps skyward
in an arc, its great body
etched against the sun.

I remember thinking
how graceless it looked,
out of its element, legs
braced and stiffened
for the plunge.

    *

They drink long
draughts, muzzles submerged
to the eyes, set out like spokes
in all directions.

The salt does its work.
First scream, proud head
thrown back, nostrils flared,
flesh tight over teeth
and gums
           (yellow teeth,
           bloody gums).
The spasms, heaving bodies,
turning, turning.

I am the centre
of this churning circumference.

The wretch beside me,
fingers
knotted to the gunwales.

*

They plunge toward
the ship, hooves crashing
on the planked hull.
Soft muzzles ripped
and bleeding on splintered wood
and barnacles.
The ensign's mare
struggles half out of the water
on the backs of two
hapless animals.

*

When the affair ended
the sea was littered with bodies,
smooth bloated carcasses.
Neither pike pole nor ship's
boats could keep them off.
Sailors that never missed
a meal retched violently
in the hot sun. Only
the silent industry of sharks
could give them rest.

*

What is the shape of freedom,
after all? Did I come here
to be devoured by insects, or
maddened by screams in the night?

Ortega, when we found him,
pinned and swinging in his bones,
jawbone pinned and singing
in the wind: God's lieutenant,
more eloquent in death.

✷

Sooner or later hope
evaporates, joy itself
is seasonal. The others?
They are Spaniards, no more
and no less, and burn with a lust
that sends them tilting
at the sun itself.

Ortega, listen, the horses,
where are the sun's horses
to pull his chariot from the sea,
end this conspiracy of dark?

The nights are long, the cold
a maggot boarding in my flesh.

✷

I hear them moving,
barely perceptible, faint
as the roar of insects.

Gathering,
gathering to thunder
across the hidden valleys
of the sea, crash of hooves
upon my door, hot quick
breath upon my face.

My eyes, he kissed my eyes,
the softness of his fingers
moving. . . .

14

*

Forgive me, I did not
mean this to be my final
offering. Sometimes the need
to forgive, be forgiven,
makes the heart a pilgrim.
I am no traveller,
my Christopher faceless
with rubbing on the voyage
out, the voyage into exile.

Islanded in our separate
selves, words
are too frail a bridge.

*

I see you in the morning
running to meet me down
the mountainside, your face
transfigured with happiness.

Wait for me, my sister,
where wind rubs bare
the cliff face, where we rode
to watch the passing ships
at daybreak, and saw them
burn golden, from masthead
down to waterline.

*

I will come soon.

from WAR & OTHER MEASURES (1976)

Book One

Standing on the escalator
at Piccadilly, she puts her hand
inside my trousers without turning.

Her body on the dirty spread
is covered with scars. She weeps
as I kiss them, her deep wound
closing around me.

I speak of Montreal.
Somehow, my being Canadian
amuses her. Our cigarettes
pencil the darkness.

In the morning she is gone,
the pillow scarred. On the floor
a spent cartridge of lipstick.

❋

Train to York in nighttime.
Frail child, legs dangling
from carriage seat, her head
an enormous wasps' nest
of bandage. And cradling
a china doll.

---

*Note: This is the first section of an imaginative recreation of the life of the
"mad bomber," Paul Joseph Chartier, who died when the dynamite he was
carrying exploded in the men's washroom of the Canadian House of
Commons on May 18, 1966.*

Tired man looks up at me,
smiles.

Badly hit, he says. Deaf, too.
Came over high, couldn't
hear until it hit. The whole house.
Doll came through without
a scratch. Fancy that.

※

Travelling by night, stopping in barns
and haystacks (no charge for the rats),
we make it, finally, behind the lines.

Guards at checkpoint, officious,
heel-clicking. Everything in order.
Fournier behind me on a bicycle.

Frightened, wanting only to run.
Walking down the road conspicuous
as a tourist, the back of my neck

grown suddenly bare. Truck stops.
So close, their soft young faces
sucking courage from a cigarette.

Surprised by my own reflection
in the windscreen, five days' growth
and wearing these filthy overalls.

I take the lift they offer.

※

Three sticks of dynamite
well placed under the jeep.
One infantry colonel, one driver,
two ambivalent authorities.

Afterward, the reprisals.
                              Twenty
townsmen, including the schoolmaster,
shot through the head, his students
attending closely to the lesson.

This is war, I say.
                              I have orders.
I have to keep moving, fear
my constant companion.

Wisdom leaking to the winds
like gas.

❋

Break the chain of command. Always
the same pattern, a child's game
of checkers: jump one, lose five.

New crop of French widows.

One more grateful than the rest
gives me food and shelter for a week.
As the husband dreams his outrage
in the parlour, I spill my grief
into her body.

Fournier found with a carving knife
in his throat. His smile
infectious, even in death.

❋

Talking to myself again,
grown more taciturn than ever
to hide the patois.

My hands fascinate me, two
live animals at my sides.

They feed me, light cigarettes,
help themselves to my things.
Night creatures, they live by day
in my pockets.

I watch them fold and unfold,
move among the objects
on the table, wonder how much
longer they will need me.

I do not want to understand
their language.

＊

Fournier's memory always amazed
me, the way he could summon up
physical detail, whole conversations,
and give them a special colouring.

He had been wandering down southside
one evening in late October, among
gutted houses, some half-standing,
when this kid materializes in a doorway
and says, *Penny for the guy, mister*,
dragging behind him a stuffed pillowcase
tied in the middle and drawn with falling
hairlock and coal-dust moustache.

Bombs intended for Westminster,
falling short, spending their fury
on the innocent. The kid crouched,
an animal alertness in his limbs,
eyes that could read a face.
Scruffy as hell — and the cheek
of his puppet Führer. Fournier used
the phrase *stuffed men of politics*
and called the kid one of those
for whom war changes nothing.

I could listen to him for hours.

*

Moon, full and uncooperative,
moving on a grid of cloud.

Running a film of my next move.
In it, I offer the sentry a smoke,
drop it. He does not rise again,
but stretches out in slow motion
among the flowers, head
twisted oddly on its broken stem.

I round the corner of the cottage,
toss two pineapples in the window
and dive for cover.

I miss the sound of his voice
already.

*

running running
somewhere to get to
trees farmhouses dumb cattle
go by me on a painted screen
someone is cranking it backstage
they're shooting again this must be
the second time around

stand of poplars can't get
past it tangled in branches
this is not fair each one
I break grows extra hands

nurse shakes me her full weight
pinning down my arms my eyes
are slow to focus she is smiling

hips draped across the bed
like a pool player's

*

this is a dream I am holding
a small child in my arms the
child's head begins to grow
arms and legs drop away its
features stretch and vanish
it becomes a globe a world
eyes staring from continents
starts to turn in my hands
floats upward past the roof
the treetops I raise my rifle
take aim there is a scream
I am covered in green paint

the doctor will like this one

*

A genuine occasion in the ward.
Two officers shaking my hand,
pinning something on my nightgown.

They smell of authority
and shoe polish, accents honed
at Oxford and Upper Canada.

My eyes remain closed. I decide
to exploit my role as screwball.
When their ritual is finished,
I release a premeditated fart,
throw the ribbon on the floor.

Everyone is embarrassed.

*

I refuse the doctor's lighter
(smell of sulphur reaches the nose
first, clings to the membranes)
and begin to talk.

Came home reeking of booze,
face puffed, small pig eyes
receding into his head.
By then she had been gone
six years, and not a letter.
Took a job as night watchman
at Eddy's, so he wouldn't
be home alone at night.

Wore his best suit to see me off
at the station, then went home
and put a match to the house.
Telegram waiting in London.
Father father, I cried, o jesus,
I loved you.

How deep do these things go,
anyway?

※

Parsons is playing *Opus Posthumous*
in the lounge again this morning.
Thinks he's poor Schubert
who died penniless at thirty-one.

I pass the window on my walk
and stop to examine a caterpillar,
also unaccompanied, making its way
across the ribwork of a leaf.

It hangs over the edge, swings
its slow body back and forth,
back, and finding nothing
withdraws its accordion shape.

Music stops. Parsons rises.
Plays well, but never gets past
the *andantino*.

✳

Funeral services held in my room
at 10:45. I invite the staff
and other patients. There are hymns,
a few prayers, and a brief eulogy
for the departed. The orderlies
wheel it out on a trolley draped
with Harris tweed, we bury it
in a matchbox. My handkerchief
is wet with smiles.

Doesn't matter what you do,
as long as you do it with style.
I used to think Fournier was queer,
he quoted Oscar Wilde so often.

✳

Today he uses my first name,
lights my cigarette, jokes
about the length people go
to get a few days off.

I tell him again of the Sutherlanders,
trekking overland from Hudson Bay,
about the thick piece of rope
from which Riel dangled.
I want to know about *you*,
he says, not your country.

My grief is an ocean
to be crossed, but it is inside,
black and fathomless.

We both pretend he understands.

✻

White sails of the nurses
glide past the open door,
a flotilla of good intentions.
Beamy, deep-keeled girls, more
stable than basic industries.

When the dust settled,
flesh of her breast lay red
and open, dark pool of blood
in the belly's hollow.
A ringed hairy finger twitches
on the hearthrug, then nothing.

Moonlight in the dead eyes
of the sentry.

from **THE ACID TEST** *(1980)*

Tower

I loved them, in my own way,
enough to pay hard cash for the rifle,
to plan my strategy long into the night.
I did not complain about the cold wind
or the exhausting climb to the tower;
even the long wait and the rank-smelling
pigeons never taxed my patience.

When they emerged, after a time,
into the bright winter sun at midday,
I spared no effort to steady the rifle,
to bring the delicate cross of the gunsights
into line with their temples or breasts.

And when they began to run, after the first
had settled to rest in the soft snow,
I never lost my cool, but took them
one by one, like a cat collecting kittens.

Sandra Lee Scheuer

(Killed at Kent State University on May 4, 1970,
by the Ohio National Guard)

You might have met her on a Saturday night
cutting precise circles, clockwise, at the Moon-Glo
Roller Rink, or walking with quick step

between the campus and a green two-storey house,
where the room was always tidy, the bed made,
the books in confraternity on the shelves.

27

She did not throw stones, major in philosophy
or set fire to buildings, though acquaintances say
she hated war, had heard of Cambodia.

In truth she wore a modicum of make-up, a brassiere,
and could, no doubt, more easily have married a
    guardsman
than cursed or put a flower in his rifle barrel.

While the armouries burned she studied,
bent low over notes, speech therapy books, pages
open at sections on impairment, physiology.

And while they milled and shouted on the commons
she helped a boy named Billy with his lisp, saying
Hiss, Billy, like a snake. That's it, SSSSSSSS,

tongue well up and back behind your teeth.
Now buzz, Billy, like a bee. Feel the air
vibrating in my windpipe as I breathe?

As she walked in sunlight through the parking lot
at noon, feeling the world a passing lovely place,
a young guardsman, who had his sights on her,

was going down on one knee as if he might propose.
His declaration, unmistakable, articulate,
flowered within her, passed through her neck,

severed her trachea, taking her breath away.
Now who will burn the midnight oil for Billy,
ensure the perilous freedom of his speech?

And who will see her skating at the Moon-Glo
Roller Rink, the eight small wooden wheels
making their countless revolutions on the floor?

Year of the Child

What did it matter, after all,
that we were careful with matches,
never dined on sleeping pills or Drano,
turned down candy and rides
even from the next-door neighbour
who was old, religious and (we thought) harmless,
kept our pencil-sharpened fingers out of sockets,
did not eat geraniums or dieffenbachia,
looked both ways for traffic
before crossing the street like somnambulists
with both arms extended,
didn't defy gravity or try to breathe underwater,
never stuck our tongues out at passing motorists
lest they be members of the Mafia on holiday,
said our prayers frequently if without fervour,
opened infant bank accounts, allowed insurance
to be taken out in our names for college,
never testified in court against our parents
or appealed the Bill of Rights.
When the time came, they hired killers
to babysit, glared at us
along gunbarrels, tossed us from windows,
doctored the Kool-Aid, set us adrift
in colanders (we mistook the mines
for bullrushes), our burst eardrums
deaf to the strains of Brahms' "Lullaby."
What did it matter, after all?
The man who pushed the button
resembled Hans Christian Andersen.

Promised Land

When I went to spy out the land
I took shin pads, gas mask,
snow tires with metal studs, radar,
bazookas, reconaissance planes,
foot powder, dental floss, FN
rifles, forged passport, a dozen
languages, hospital insurance
and a jock strap with a metal cup.

On my way to case the land
I took Batman comics, walkie-talkie,
hand grenades and bayonets, a yoyo,
the memory of mother waving clean socks
and underwear, life insurance,
the *Encyclopaedia Britannica*, Moses'
blessing, a cassette, a mickey of rye,
antihistamine, a few addresses,
bongo drums, *Playboy*, equipment
for wiretaps, green garbage bags,
Kleenex, laxative, an inflatable raft,
pemmican, flares, corn plasters,
return tickets, spare batteries,
contraceptives, an atlas.

I knew this was the right place,
I sold the whole lot the first day.

THE TERRACOTTA ARMY (1984)

Charioteer

So they call you layabouts a standing army?
There's more life in this terracotta nag

than in the whole first division. With that
Bi leapt on the back of a cavalry pony he had fired

the previous day and dug his heels into the outline
of ribs. I wouldn't have been surprised

to see it leap into action and clear the doorway
with the potter shouting death to the enemy.

Most of the animals were cast from a single mould
and could be distinguished one from the other

only by the application of paint and dyes. I took
exception to this and remarked that, as charioteer,

I found more distinctive characteristics in horses
than in men. Bi swung his legs over the neck

and dropped to the ground. He was no taller
than the ponies he fashioned. Then, with a flourish,

he drew a green moustache on the horse's muzzle
and fell about the pottery amused by his own joke.

Note: Approximately eight thousand underground pottery soldiers, constructed for the first Emperor of China, Ch'in Shi Huang, as protection in the afterlife, were discovered by accident near Xian in 1974.

Spearman

Before double-ninth day, my measure was taken
in a single sitting, so sure were Lao Bi's

eye and hand. The tenth month I returned
with armoured vest and spear and struck a pose

that pleased him so much he laughed out loud
and threw his wineskin at my feet.

He called me the youngest of the Immortals
and promised me a place in the glory-line.

The likeness was uncanny, not just the face,
but the way the sleeves bunched up at the wrists,

studs and fluted leather of the shoulder pads.
I was drawn to it again and again as if by magic.

One day, without warning, we left for the frontier
and I felt a greater reluctance

to part with this pottery replica of myself
than I had in taking leave of my own village.

Bi used to slap me on the back and say,
you're too serious to be a soldier.

Guardsman

At first I did not like him and put it down
to the arrogance of the creative mind,

his not mine. I'd been the previous day,
guarding the entrance to Ch'in Shi Huang's tomb,

where the artisans and craftsmen were at work
fashioning god knows what final luxuries

for the imperial afterlife. By the sounds of it,
they were feeling no pain. I mentioned this

quite casually, by way of small talk,
to the master potter as he examined my skull

and he exploded like a devil, threatening
to cut off my head for more detailed study.

Needless to say, I wasted no time absenting myself
from his presence and stopped in for a drink

at my quarters. They told me the tomb was finished
and the great door had been dropped into place,

sealing in every artist and workman employed there.
My hands flew, of their own accord, to cover my throat.

Minister of War

I was a young man on the make, a brain for hire,
a travelling politician. I saw my chance,

adopted Ch'in, advised the death of feudal tenure,
not to mention purges and the burning of books.

I scorned the golden mean of men like Mencius
and learned my politics from rats in the latrine;

yet I had respect enough for the written word to know
that old records and systems are better destroyed

than left to seed rebellion and discontent in the period
of transition. The same logic applied to scholars

33

and authors, those masters of anamnesis, or recall.
I kept the emperor occupied with toy soldiers

and the arts, or fears of death and court intrigue,
while the real politics unfolded as I knew it would:

highways, taxes, centralization, promotion by exam.
He might have stopped my war against the past,

but I saw to the depths of his and all men's hearts,
where artist lies down, at last, with bureaucrat.

Lieutenant

You might call me a jack-of-all-the-arts;
I paint, draw maps, sing, write a fair poem.

I skipped basic training because of the length
of my tongue and managed to nab a commission

right away in the reserve. I can toss off a lyric
or forge an epic in a single afternoon,

still observing the unities. Once I entered
the emperor's competition and almost made it

to the finals. As far as visual arts are concerned,
I'm no slouch either. I've been known to sketch

enemy encampments in pitch black, still mounted,
give an accurate impression of slaughter

on the battlefield, avoiding dangerous skirmishes
and ignoring cries for help in order to complete

my precious record. The potter was not impressed.
Learn to write with this, he said, positioning

my hands on the jade hilt of an ornate sword,
the enemy has not yet learned to read.

Paymaster

We stood beside the trenches and looked at the rows
of figures there, bronze horses harnessed in gold

and silver, some of the charioteers in miniature
with robes and hairstyles denoting superior rank;

then the pottery horses with their snaffle bits
and bridles of stone beads. These had been fired

in one piece, except for the tail and forelock.
Most of the men could be seen to wear toques

over their topknots. Kang, of course, had abandoned
such fashions and stood there with an eternal leer

and his pot-belly showing through armour, rivets
forever about to pop. A sensualist I was astounded

as usual by the loving attention to detail and asked Bi
what thoughts this assembled spectacle called up in him.

Counterfeit currency, he said. A life's work
that will never be seen, poems tossed in bonfires.

A poem lives on in the ear, but a single push
will topple all of these.

Infantryman

We all marvelled at the courage of Ching K'o,
a serious man of letters who loved books

and often drank to excess with dog butchers
and lute players in the marketplace.

To please the Crown Prince Tan of Yen, who feared
the imminent demise of his kingdom by Ch'in,

Ching K'o agreed to undertake a daring plot
to assassinate the emperor. Delivering the head

of Ch'in's hated enemy General Fan in a box,
Ching K'o unrolled a map of the Yen territories

to be ceded. When the concealed dagger appeared,
Ching K'o snatched it up and grabbed the sleeve

of the emperor, but the cloth tore in his hand
and his advantage was lost. Bi laughed

at this turn of events and made some remark
about the advantages of shoddy workmanship.

We tended to ignore his smart-ass comments
and asides, but the irony was not lost on us.

Mess Sergeant

It was not so much the gossip that attracted me
to Bi's pottery, though there was plenty of that:

news of the latest atrocities against the people,
rights and property abolished, heads of children

staring vacantly from terraces, dismembered corpses
turning slowly in the current along the north bank

of the Wei. Rather it was a sort of clearing-house,
a confessional, where our greatest fears were exorcised

piecemeal through the barter of objective detail.
I remember the day when word came of the taking

of Yen. Streets ran with the colour of Ch'in's revenge.
The lute player, Kao-Chien Li, who had plucked Ching K'o

on his way to assassinate the emperor, was blinded
and forced to serenade the victors without ceasing,

blood still running down his face and arms.
Not a sound was heard in the pottery, except the crackle

of logs burning and the sizzle of spit as the last
moisture escaped from the baking clay figures.

Military Historian

And so he standardized everything — axes, measures,
even the language itself. Six of this,

six of that, the uniform evils of power.
What can you say about a man who would burn

books and the keepers of books? So great
was his fear of chaos and the unknown

he was a dupe for any kind of mumbo-jumbo
and excess. One of the wily magicians at court

convinced Ch'in he could find the fabled Island
of Immortals, but must take along the price

not only of gold and silver in great abundance,
but also a host of beautiful youths of both sexes.

Ch'in complied. Nothing more was heard of them.
The emperor put out that they were lost at sea,

but others amongst us presumed the magician
had set himself up nicely on the islands of Fu Sang.

All this came to light much later, when Ch'in
died at the coast, vainly looking out to sea.

Blacksmith

Bi remarked on the lethal aspect of the crossbow,
whose trigger mechanism I'd just improved.

Tests had been done that morning on criminal types
who'd failed to comply with laws on standardization.

At short range the crossbow sent a heavy arrow
through the breasts of five men with surprisingly little

loss of speed; it was equally efficient on two others
in full armour, standing back to back outside the gates

of the A-fang palace. I received a rousing cheer
from the assembled soldiers and nobility;

even the castratos pressed into service in the grounds
and gardens seemed more than slightly impressed.

Bi was sweating profusely and I thought he looked
rather pale in the dim light as he worked on details

of the armoured vest of a kneeling crossbowman.
Where is the dragon, rain-bringer, lord of waters

when we need him, the potter muttered to himself,
wiping the blade of the chisel on his leather apron.

Harness-Maker

The plot to assassinate Ch'in Shi Huang
was a regular topic at the pottery.

Bi used it as an occasion to sound off about one
or other of his pet theories. What did I tell you,

he said one morning, unwrapping the four bridles
I had just delivered, a man who hangs out

with drunkards and ne'er-do-wells can't be all bad, eh?
No wonder his royal highness never sleeps in the same

bed two nights in a row. And his concubines —
what a waste! How can a man with so much on his mind

keep up his standard of performance? I have it
in strictest confidence from the younger sister

of his current favourite that, contrary to legend,
the Tiger of Ch'in is nothing but a pussycat.

Talk of this sort was confined to a trusted few,
including several peasants who made daily deliveries

of wood and bricks. One, brother of conscript Ch'en She,
squatted like a coiled spring in the corner, grinning.

Strategist

Avoid precipitous cliffs, marshes, quagmires, thickets;
at all times, make the terrain work to your advantage.

Arrive first and lie in wait, rested, fully alert.
Tempt the enemy into the open with shows of weakness.

Don't neglect spies, alliances, the impact of banners, gongs,
drums; detach a flying column, if needed, for a rout.

Better yet, win the war without fighting at all.
Information's the thing. What weapon or scaling device

can replace the trained ear? Nothing, at least
not in my books. There is no sure defence against a good

pair of eyes. The Five Factors can remain constant,
and the Five Year Plans, but what are the economies of war

when increased levies exhaust a people's substance
and spirit and bring the aggressor to his knees

before the enemy? Remember, prolonged war is folly;
so, too, is laying siege to a walled city.

Without these principles the whole empire, not just
the imperial army, will be in ruins.

Spy

I'd read Sun Tzu,
that was my mistake,

read his *Art of War*
and committed it to memory.

Li Ssu was impressed; otherwise,
he might have left me alone

tending what few books remained
in the imperial library.

I was without status, no beauty either,
nondescript, down at the heels,

nobody's idea of a good time.
But I had my uses.

I was designated Category Five,
the surviving spy,

and ambled freely between the court
and Bi's establishment,

letting my body go to pot
but not my cover.

Commando

My youngest brother disappeared without a trace
after the first recruitment. He was a musician

of no small promise, had anyone bothered to inquire,
and might have piped the hearts of simple men

to final victory or wrapped their deadly wounds in notes
of purest silk. Did he lend his flesh to the rubble

of a wall or make his bones instruments of war?
Don't ask. The new carts rattled by on their standard

axles, half-empty. Next they bred a line
of uniform slaves. Forced labour and conscription

destroyed the base of agriculture, brought revolt.
Who's to say it wasn't for the best?

You can tell by the lightness of my armour
I'm a crack trooper, trained to take the initiative

in battle. I prayed daily my strength would win
sufficient honours to bring me into the presence

of Ch'in and his bloody councillor, to strike
a chord that's truly worthy of my brother.

Unarmed Footsoldier

Education does not win battles or put bread
on the table. I was a student once, I know.

I had my champions, my favourite causes;
the afternoons I was not gallivanting in full heat,

I spent debating the meaning of the universe.
Why did I bother? There's nothing quite like war

to clear the head — or remove it. I was drafted,
I became the perfect machine, precision tool

for the mechanics of death. I was programmed
to kill. I did not need spear or crossbow:

a well-placed blow would kill an ox or man
instantly; my special kick was called

the eunuch-maker. Still, my previous studies
were not entirely in vain. I was able to apply

the psychology I'd learned to outwitting the enemy
and, of course, my rivals within the ranks.

The potter read my story to the letter:
poised, unbalanced, deadly hollow.

Captain of the Guard

Is there no aesthetic consistency anymore,
that's what I want to know.

I registered a complaint, after the first sitting,
that he had taken more time braiding the tail

of a cavalry pony and stippling the sandals
of a kneeling warrior than he had taken

getting the fine detail of this face, which
has turned more than pottery heads in its time.

The next thing I know he's placed the head
of that ugly recruit, now bearded, on the six-foot

frame of an officer and recorded for posterity
my untrimmed growth of whiskers.

No, I don't think it was the booze, at least
not primarily. A man like that creates

his own demons and opiates. Realist or formalist —
choose your poison. Was Ch'in drunk

when he shaved a mountain that had thwarted him
and had it painted red, as a warning to all nature?

Unit Commander

I was never too keen about the shape of my ears,
the way they hang there like two horseshoes

someone had stuck on as an afterthought.
So I can't say I was anxious to be duplicated

by this barbarous southerner, whose words fell
about my feet like shards, kiln-dried and jagged.

We talked at length about Ch'in's appropriations,
not just the women, art and slaves

acquired from the defeated princes, but also designs
of palaces and gardens ordered to be copied

and reproduced in Hsienyang, as if a man
might live in more than one house at a time.

He raged against the slipperiness of Immortals,
even immortal rats in their underground mazes;

then he went on, too long according to my notes,
about lack of imagination among peoples of the north,

how even into death they must carry a representation
of the living world. I couldn't believe my ears.

Quartermaster

Seize reality in the act,
embrace its opposites like a lover,

without moderation. That's the ticket.
Though the flesh be captive,

insurgent thoughts invade the palace grounds,
storm the reviewing stand. Freedom is born

in the anarchy of spilled blood.
Did I say that, or was it Master Bi?

He spoke so close to my ear as he applied
the clay to mould my features that his ideas

washed over my brain as if I were a puppet.
Certainly I don't remember propositions

of that sort troubling my professional self,
whose sole task was the dispensing of goods,

not words: weapons, food, clothing, rivets, lumber,
and sundry items for the conduct of war.

And no one ever came to my tent and said:
Hey, buddy, give me a new idea, size five-and-a-half.

Archer

He told me the emperor's eunuch had paid a visit,
then Ch'in Shi Huang himself, disguised

as a standard-bearer. I was half-mad with curiosity
to know what had transpired between them; instead,

I made some joke about the Great Ch'in
apprenticing to a potter. Bi mimed the action

of the crossbow and told me I was on target
as usual. Damn it, he shouted,

the man is hedging his imperial bets!
He knows he'll be judged by the company he keeps,

even underground. I told him I had neither power
nor inclination to fashion a god, simple as that.

Never mind, it's done. He's given me a month
to reconsider, while he swims and scans the seas

for some immortal vessel. Here Bi took my hand
in his terrible grip as if it had been an injured

bird. I felt his breath on my face as he spoke:
A man must know where his destiny lies, eh?

Lookout

For days he could not be found and was rumoured
to have returned to his boyhood home near Guilin,

where he had been a fisherman. Others claimed
he was sleeping off a drunk. Nothing was mentioned,

but his hand seemed less steady and his eyes
had a faraway look. Don't consider it odd if I dwell

overlong on your face, he said, it is perhaps my last
and will accompany me to the land of the White Snake.

He asked if I believed in astrology and practised
the lively arts. I told him I was a simple lookout

who could spot signs of movement a long way off
and keep a warning beacon alive in all kinds of weather

but, beyond that, I had no theories or opinions.
It occurred to me he might be a bit deranged,

what with working near all that heat and fumes.
Then he told me things about myself that scared me

and some that sent me back thinking I wasn't such a bad
chap, after all. You can't fault a man for that.

Regimental Drummer

He refused, of course, to acknowledge the likeness
and huffed a good deal when I mentioned it.

I supposed he had a cousin in the imperial guard
but recalled a conversation weeks before

when he'd claimed to have no living relatives.
This is my family now, he'd added, pointing

to several terracotta figures in the corner.
But there wasn't the slightest doubt;

this unarmed soldier, turned slightly to reduce
the target area, legs apart, hands ready to parry

or strike a blow, was none other than Bi himself.
Portrait of the artist as master of martial arts,

in the front line, ready for anything, even his warts
rescued from oblivion. We drank a lot of wine

that night and danced around the pottery, reciting
poems and beating drums for the unsung dead.

A slight smile played about the lips and I found myself
winking at the copy instead of the original.

General

If this is what we have evolved toward,
I have to laugh. The illusion of full knowledge

gave us a sinister edge; we soon became
the crassest of materialists and would tolerate

neither doubt nor disturbing hypothesis. In a word,
vulgar. How easily the innocent joy of the enthusiast

gives way to the intolerance of the true believer.
We began, like all the others, with a vision:

unification, call it what you will. The sorcery
of a fixed idea. For this we marched long years,

long miles, until, winning the war, we found we had
lost face. We became the new reactionaries,

eliminating, in short order, all the best minds.
Not all things are dangerous to the body politic;

being the son of a farmer, I should have remembered
that certain organisms must not only be allowed,

but also actively cultivated. Nature can be studied,
but never controlled or predicted with absolute precision.

Minister of War

It's not because of superior rank or position
I'm allotted extra space to speak.

I merely have twice as much to answer for.
I was the right hand of God, responsible

for carrying out the wishes of the leader.
I grew to be more than a soldier, or less —

48

a politician, which the potter describes cleverly
as a freak of nature that soars above the crowd

but still has ears close to the ground. Of course
I liked Master Bi. We were inextricably linked

by our humour and intelligence. He spoke in riddles
to confound the wise, but also to spread unrest

among the rank and file. I had plans, my own art
to pursue. I exercised decorum,

arranged for another artist to betray him.
Records were kept, tongues

loosed in the usual ways. The plot,
discovered, required a dénouement.

Chaplain

Someone will break us of the habit of war
by taking away our weapons

and we will march against the darkness
(or will it be light?) naked as newborn babes,

our tiny fists opening and closing on nothing.
The only certainty, even under the earth,

is change, whether it be cosmetic, paint
flaking away down the muted centuries,

or something more violent that destroys the form
itself, icons of public and private selves.

With such thoughts I addressed the potter
on more than one occasion, thinking to shock him.

I'd given up the Tao and had even less time
for the ethics of Confucius in the new dispensation.

Rituals and ancestor worship are as useless to soldiers
as scapulimancy and tortoise-shell prophecy.

Only our vanity is monumental, the potter said,
and that, too, can be broken.

Standard Bearer

Who remembers names or issues now?
The wall that taxed us to the limits

stopped neither time nor barbarians.
Birds flew freely over the battlements,

testing the currents of non-aligned air;
so, too, did the arrows of our adversaries.

Then the enemy himself learned to fly
by subtle propaganda into our hearts

or by invention into our very midst,
wreaking havoc like a berserker.

I joined the potter in his rest;
I broke his ranks but could not break his will.

Only our forms endure. And stubborn words
which hover and adhere attend our passing

like faithful retainers. Remnants
of an age when the mind groped its way

in darkness, without maps of logic or conquest,
sweeping in its wake the relentless dust.

from CHANGES OF STATE (1986)

The Strap

No other sound was heard throughout the school
as Jimmy Bunn surrendered to the strap.
He stood before me in the counsellor's office
eye to eye, while the desk drawer gaped,
his farmer's hands stretched out in turn
expectant as beggars. My heart was touched.
I gave them more than they had bargained for.
Six on each. The welts, like coins,
inflated as we watched. Nothing he'd done
deserved such largesse, disrupting my sermon
on the Bay of Pigs invasion and how Americans
are hooked on violence, etcetera, etcetera.
They say there's a kinship in aggression
that knits the torturer and his victim;
we came to be the best of friends.
But each excuse and subterfuge exploded
in my brain as he dropped his puffed pink hams
and fought back tears. I put the leather tongue
into the gaping drawer and pushed it shut.

Jimmy's Place

We found the cow in a grove below the road,
leaning against an alder for support,
her udder swollen, her breath ragged and grating
as a rasp. I could have drowned
in the liquid eye she turned to me.
Her calf, though dead, was perfectly positioned,
forelegs and head protruding from the flaming ring
of vulva. Too large, perhaps, or hind legs
broken through the sac, dispersing fluids.

51

Much as we tried we couldn't pry it loose
and the flesh around the legs began to give
from pressure on the rope. The cow
had no more strength and staggered back
each time we pulled. Tie her to the tree,
I said, being the schoolmaster and thinking
myself obliged to have an answer, even here
on the High Road, five miles south of town
where the island bunched in the jumble
of its origins. It was coming, by God,
I swear it, this scrub roan with her shadow self
extending out behind, going in both directions
like a '52 Studebaker, coming by inches
and our feet slipping in the mud and shit
and wet grass. She raised her head and tried
to see what madness we'd concocted in her wake,
emitted a tearing gunny-sack groan,
and her liquid eye ebbed back to perfect white.

Saskatchewan: 1949

Father is riding
the ridgepole of the new barn
and dreaming ocean.

He grips the keel
with shipwright's thighs.
Studs and two-by-fours
like bleached white ribs
take measure of the sky.

He cannot fathom the wash
of tides, war's currents,
love's *coups d'état*,
that ground him
on this ancient seabed
of prairie.

He knows
what his fingers know:
claw hammer, crowbar,
and a clutch of nails.

Close-hauled bedsheets
nudge the house to windward.
Ripe wheat breaks like surf
on beaches of new lumber.

Ahoy! Ahoy! cries Noah
from his ark.

Shoals of brown cattle
dot the sweetgrass shallows.
Crows swim up like sturgeon
from the startled corn.

The Dump

Here's Rhéal, speaking of God
at the edge of the dump,
air so blue
even the flies are shocked.

A man picking among ruins
may, after all, find truth
among its substitutes.

Each day the traps are set
for small creatures
attracted to the dump.
They leave their coats behind
or stay, more stuffed than ever
to decorate the patched schoolbus.
Snowy owls officiate inside

and squirrels in multicoloured tartans
mimic a final fling.

This God of yours, Rhéal,
is an exacting mathematician,
who calculates the sum of his ecstacies
and calls it love.

Time gnaws our bones.
Centuries scavenge in the finite dust
to be remembered.
The rubbish poets talk
will end up here as well
with discarded pots, family albums.

Viens icitte, my friend,
we'll toast the nuns
who beat you mercilessly as a child,
placed their fine black boots on your neck
and applied, repeatedly, to your ass
the yardstick with its trinity of feet.
Thus you took measure of them
and their religion,
cursed them roundly till the joy
withered beneath their nightly habits.

The yellow bus is going nowhere.
Its small wood heater
pulses like a heart.

Weather

When bluejays
hang around an apple tree
you know a storm
is coming.

That's John
who sees more
with his one good eye
than most of the neighbours
with their education
and tinted lenses.

The radio confirms
a drop in temperature
of 35 degrees
before nightfall.

John drops a pinch of tobacco
onto the cigarette paper
and worries it into shape,
passing the paper twice
across his tongue.

Sometimes I think
he's pulling my leg
and the damaged eye
is merely locked
in a permanent wink.
Still, I watch the dogs
in summer, believing
if they chew grass
rain will come.
And if the chickens
hadn't been eaten by the dogs
I'd watch them too
for predictions
of shower or rain all day.

Now we're quiet, words
superfluous in the wood heat
from trees John has cut.
Year's end. The earth turns
in his presence, seasons
stand quietly in line.

John stirs to go.
Outside, the fenced pasture
fills with snow.

Tomorrow I'll come east
to blow your driveway.

Out thoughts gather
in a drawer in Cornwall hospital
where the glass eye waits
in molded styrofoam,
unseeing, unremembering,

nothing to report.

Philip Larkin

He was a man whose words stopped short
of ecstasy, whose impaired tongue and ear refused
the grand theme, the gesture of extravagance,
and found, instead, out along the side-roads,

pantleg rolled, cycle propped against a tree,
a desperation so quietly profound even toad,
blinking among grass-spears, had overlooked.
He composed no score for happiness, but improvised

a life of common pleasures taken in a minor key:
a few pints with friends who didn't talk of poetry,
an early morning stroll in Pearson Park,
industrialist's gift to dreary, fog-bound Hull,

sausages on campus, a slice of Humber pie.
Hearing aid turned off, he tunes his inner music,
private soul station, some such jazz,
communes with Jelly Roll and Beiderbecke,

and watches from his window at the Nuffield,
where Westbourne intersects with Salisbury,
winos rub themselves against the freshly painted
thighs of mermaids in the Victorian fountain,

who take their own libations from a conch.
While such doleful enthusiasts drink his health,
all flesh conspires to silence Larkin;
he undergoes a sea-change in the Avenues.

With no more reason to attend, he sings the poem
of his departure, achieves his wish to be alone.
Propped up in bed and talking to himself,
one thing only is denied: the desire of oblivion.

The Last Canto

I seldom budge
from Rapallo.
Venice is no Byzantium
these final days.
Stench from the canals
worse than the cattle ship
I sailed to Europe on.

Mr Nixon was half right:
poetry did not pay,
but there was a future in it.
The age demanded
a scapegoat and a saint.
Being American
I applied for both jobs.

The world has been my whale-road,
wanderer and seafarer
among the lost manuscripts,
charting connections

few had even dreamed of.
I've gone about my business
like a pack rat.
You have to do that,
have on hand ten times
what you can ever hope to use.
Tennyson was right
about being part of all he met,
but he hadn't met enough.

As the range broadened
my speech became barbarous,
that of a man who's lost contact
with the words of his fellows,
though he knows their hearts'
most intimate desires.

I once advised trashing the metronome
and composing with the music
of the speaking voice.
Now I say:
Exercise the mind
and school the heart;
voice will rejoice
in its tender chains
like a bridegroom.

While my former countrymen
have given up on ideas,
except in things,
whatever that means,
and play with themselves
like clergymen,
less out of need than habit,
I dream
of ideas in action
and of forma, even the canetto,
where the dance of ear
and intellect

draw dormant filings
into the pattern of a rose.

I wrote in an article
in *T.P's Weekly* in 1913:
The artist is always beginning.
Any work of art
which is not a beginning,
an invention, a discovery,
is of little worth.

I still hold that view
though at times, I admit,
I counted the cost.

I have spoken too much of usura,
or not enough.
Even the air we breathe
is rented for a price.

Forget my dicta:
direct treatment of the thing
and all that rot.
The thing, so-called,
has yet to be revealed.
I have found poems
to be wiser and more honest
than poets.

Remember the ideogram
from the Chinese,
the one representing truth
which shows a man
standing beside his word.
Nothing more.
The merchant's wife
dying alone
in her unkempt garden
by the river

praises
my irregular feet,
though she draws the line
at Social Credit.

Forget me too:
listen to the poems.

You see, I'm prescriptive
to the end, a weakness
acquired in Hailey, Idaho
and never shaken.

Mahatma Gandhi Refuses An Invitation to Write for Reader's Digest

Gentlemen:

celibacy, in the extreme,
is no less violent
than sex

blood is thicker
than the briny, clichéd waters
of Chowpatty Beach
but religion will prove
thicker than both

a man's life
cannot be condensed
to a series of major scenes
in lighted boxes
without distortion

nor did the letter of an obscure
Indian lawyer

secure the release
of Sacco & Vanzetti

Tagore, as he sits beside me
in the wicker armchair,
waiting to be photographed,
appears massive, twice my size,
yet there's no denying
the delicacy and grace
of the manuscript
he holds awkwardly in his lap
or the confidence
he has given the people
in their roots

the dead woman in the street
outside the railway station
in Bombay is not there
to provoke the curiosity
or guilt of tourists

there are wounds
no amount of salt can heal
regardless of the manufacturer

Indigestibly yours

To the Women of the Fo Shan Silk Commune

What sailor rounding the Horn
or camel driver navigating
the tortuous mountain passes
does not come to a quiet harbour
or oasis in his thoughts,
where he can hear the bombyx moths
feed upon leaves of mulberry,
spinning their silken threads

or filaments, and see your smooth arms
twist and weave a destiny
he might once have entered, deep
in the shadows of the old mill
where his master, like some machine
or abacus, clicked out prices and quantities
without error, as if the heart
required no other raiment?
You sit amidst the merciless clamour of the looms
dealing happiness and longevity
in gold characters into the cloth,
while the membranes grow dull
and die within your ears.
Listen to me, read my lips:
there are none so deaf
as those who will not hear.
Come to your senses!
The lotus, I say, is not more lovely
or more delicate. I want you
to wake in the silent dawn
to hear your lover slip into his clothes
and shut the door behind him so gently
his departure is no more than a sigh.
I want the hush of that moment
to ring in your ears all day like a shout
of triumph, a call to arms.
Fear not the transformations you must face,
changes of state.
The cocoon of love arrests you
for a time in its silken embrace.
You will endure it. You will emerge,
your smile threadbare but intact.
A new beauty awaits you
at every turn.

The Uses of Poetry

Among workers at the Daxing Ivory Factory
there's a man carving an ivory ball
that will take seven months to complete
and contain, in its milky depths,
over forty free-moving spheres.
Several women artists are at work
on composite landscapes
of people, animals and trees.
One holds a block of ivory in her hands
from which two lovers emerge,
heads and shoulders released from captivity
by the dreaming eye and skilful hand.
Nothing is wasted. Even the dust
is used for medicinal purposes,
boiled in water and served as a treatment
for fever and teething in infants.
Finally, I'm introduced to Feng,
the master craftsman and senior artist,
perched on his stool near the window,
where he transcribes T'ang poems
on the flat end of a fragment of ivory
no larger than a toothpick.
The characters are so minute
they must be read with magnifying glass.
Later, at dinner, the poets will scoff
at this ancient bourgeois practice
and declare their preference
for books and broadcast.
In my country, where poems
are seldom found in bookstores
or on the lips of small children,
I wonder who'll preserve them
for a caring age. What are the uses
of poetry? To launch a purge,
promote another product? Surely
not the oblivion of the marketplace
or media. Something to carry in a wallet

to clean your teeth or savour
for a moment, perhaps, in private
before the government changes
or the clock stops. Nothing justifies
the slaughter of elephants or innocents,
certainly not poetry. But let there be
always someone in a small room
above the street and its tragedies,
whose mind and hand recall us
in our gentler moments,
when we had time to carve our dreams
and initials on a tree trunk
or a piece of bone,
that amongst the rubble
as the legions pass, some soldier
may see, magnified a hundred times
through broken glass, these words
of fire and wind.

from HONG KONG (1987)

Gyselman

Among the documents
you'll find a picture of me
standing on a railway tie
at the Winnipeg station,
a cigarette in my fingers.

The puff of smoke I exhale
looks like Scotch thistle
on my tunic lapel.
My face has the arrogant leer
of an evangelist.

Two months later
a quarter of us would be wounded
or dead and I'd dream nightly
of rats eating dead Japanese.

Kravinchuk

We're out back
of the reservoir
when this Nip plane
comes over the ridge
and opens fire.

Note: On October 26, 1942, 1,975 soldiers of the Winnipeg Grenadiers and the Royal Rifles of Canada were sent to defend Hong Kong against impossible odds; untrained and ill-equipped, they were quickly defeated by crack Japanese troops. To losses in battle were added the casualties of brutal POW camps and, later, the unwillingness of the Canadian government to grant the survivors proper benefits and care.

As the shells hit
a trail of dust-devils
snakes towards us
across the valley.
We stand gaping
like a couple of yokels
until it's just about
overhead, then dive
into the makeshift bunker.
Harris starts screaming
I'm hit, I'm hit,
O God, Sam, you can
feel the warm blood
on my shoulder.
His tragic look
is so authentic
you'd think
he'd rehearsed it
from old movies.
He'd have run off
screaming like that, too,
if I hadn't grabbed
both his ankles
and shouted:
Tea, you stupid fucker,
tea. I spilled the thermos
down your back.

Henderson

I did most of my fighting in Repulse Bay
in a hotel half-full of civilians.
We took up positions in a plush suite
on the second floor.

One of the men sat in an armchair
scanning hills out back with binoculars.

When he spotted movement, I'd swing
into the window and fire, then drop back.

Suddenly there was a woman in the doorway,
saying, My dog, I'm looking for water for my dog.
We pulled her down out of the line of fire
and gave the dog radiator water we used for tea.

Later, when the Japanese were two football fields away
and their planes were dive-bombing the barracks,
I thought of that woman and her parting comment:
If he bothers you by barking, shoot him.

Sullivan

There's a strange hush at St. Stephen's
as we wait for them to storm the college.
Nurses drift like butterflies among the injured,
offering a word, a touch, a cigarette.
When the enemy bursts through the door

I'm lying on a cot at the far end of the corridor,
my head bandaged, my leg supported in a sling.
Two soldiers proceed to bayonet the sick and wounded
in their beds, to a chorus of screams and protests.
A nurse throws herself on top of one of our boys

to protect him — it might have been the kid
from Queen's — and they are both killed
by a single thrust of the bayonet.
I suppose they were sweethearts. Pinned
at last, she does not struggle. Her hands

open and close once, like tiny wings,
and the dark stain on her white, starched uniform
spreads like a chrysanthemum, a blood-red sun.
I cut the cord supporting my leg, slip on
the nearest smock and stand foolishly at attention,

making the salute. My right index finger
brushes the damp cotton of the bandage.
Later, the butchers are shot by their own officers;
one, apparently, had lost a brother
in the final assault.

Four

I spent several mornings in the offices of the *South China
Morning Post*, reading copies of *Hong Kong News* produced
after the Japanese victory on Christmas Day in 1941. Early
sun glinted off the high-rises and office towers in Victoria as
I crossed on the Star Ferry and a huge Bayer Aspirin sign on
the roof of a building confirmed my impression of the Crown
Colony as a colossal headache.

I was staying in an unheated room in Chungking Man-
sions on Nathan Road, Kowloon-side, a high-rise slum that
offered a rich assortment of internationals selling silk, sex, and
semiprecious gems. Ascending in the creaking elevator, you
witnessed a discontinuous film-strip of erotic tableaux, heated
arguments, and half-finished transactions.

The cluster of rooms on the seventh floor was bucolic by
contrast and had an air of exhausted camaraderie that sur-
prised me, a tribute to the two families of Chinese who ran
the place. My room looked out on an alley, a dark, awesome
abyss that separated me from the balconies and opulent
suites of the Holiday Inn. For only four dollars a night, I could
switch my lights off and, unobserved from my window, watch
the comings and goings in those expensive rooms. Or I
could gaze at the stars through a cloud cover of laundry
hanging out to dry on the floor above.

I soon tired of both astrology and low-grade voyeurism
and made the rounds of the local bars, particularly the Ship's
Inn, run by a Vietnam veteran who'd parlayed his injuries
and discharge into a small fortune on the black market. He'd
also developed certain tastes only the Orient could satisfy.

Jim was curious about my mission in Hong Kong, gather-
ing information about Canadians killed or incarcerated there

during the war. He ventured it was only non-combatants
who wrote about the war. I nursed my glass of bitters and
thought of Wilfred Owen, Charles Yale Harrison, even the
Royal Rifles' own William Allister. Jim's stitch-marks ran
from one ear down across his throat to the other shoulder,
like a tiny rope ladder on a helicopter. I said I supposed he
was probably right.

Six

The prime minister knew what Churchill said
concerning the defence of Hong Kong.
He wrote the words more or less verbatim
in his diary:

> Let us devote ourselves to what is possible.
> Japan will take Hong Kong, beyond the shadow
> of a doubt, when the time comes. Think
> only of a presence.

Symbolic garrison, that was
the operative phrase.

But he knew, also, the words
of a mother in Moose Jaw
who would not release the hand
he extended until he heard
her thoughts about the war:
a farm dying from neglect
while husband and son
rot in the Yorkshire rain.

He did not bother to tell her
they were among the ranks
that booed his presence
on parade in England.
He saw blood. Privately,
of course. And it was blood

69

he knew would bring them round
to the war effort, the blood
of mothers' sons
spilled on foreign soil.

So he gave the nod to Crerar
and prayed forgiveness
from his dearest Mum.

Distinguished Service Decorations

Pellagra
is a vitamin-deficiency disease
that produces sores on the skin,
red and weeping sores, as well as ulcers
on the lips, gums, tongue and throat.

It also has a tendency to cause
severe irritation and chafing
around the genitals. Thus
the nickname: Rice Balls
and Strawberry Balls.

The three Ds of pellagra are
dermatitis, diarrhoea, dementia.

Mallory

Work party at 6 a.m. Low-flying fog over the harbour as we
board the ferry that takes us from Shamshuipo to Kai Tak.
Bitter cold. Can see only the Peak over Victoria now. No won-
der money builds high up, a hedge against fire, flood, disease,
the poor.

I'm working alongside Delisle, who can barely raise his
shovel, never mind sing in his perfect tenor voice. The poor
devil has been down in sick-bay for weeks with dysentery

and electric feet. The grey skin is stretched over his bones like kite paper. I try to cover for him by working a little faster than usual, but I know I can't keep up the pace. There must be a hundred of us working on the Reclamation, dumping earth from high ground to extend the runway into the sea. You have to keep moving or freeze.

"Dummy, speedo!" The guards are shouting to our left, trying to make better time. I suppose they get more rations if the work goes well and a few extra inches are gained each day.

I fill Delisle's baskets as lightly as I can and help him up with them. He moves off ahead of me, so thin he looks as if he might crumble under the weight. The concentration required to put one foot ahead of the other must be enormous, but he plods toward the fabricated shoreline. He's not quite over the dysentery and the backs of his legs are stained from the thin bile that passes through him. He resembles a mechanical scale, the two baskets suspended from the ends of a pole at slightly different levels at his sides.

If we can make it to the edge without attracting attention, no one will notice the size of his load. We're only twenty yards from the water when one basket dips below knee-level and brushes the ground. It's just enough to betray him. He falls straight forward on his face. The wicker baskets, unfortunately, remain upright and reproachful beside him.

I stand at attention, my legs aching under the weight. Delisle does not move. I think his heart has given out, but I hear him whisper.

"Je m'excuse, Alvin. Je m'excuse."

Two guards are kicking and shouting. They drag him to his feet and knock him back and forth between them like a rag doll. One of them reaches into a half-filled basket and throws a handful of dirt into Alvin's face. The closed eyes seem to infuriate him as much as the baskets.

"Dummy, cheat. No good."

Delisle's bowels choose this moment to discharge, though he has eaten nothing for days. It's a miracle of creation, or criticism. *Ex nihilo fecit.* The guard's face contorts and he strikes Delisle in the mouth with his rifle butt. Then they are dragging him to the water's edge.

All work on the Reclamation has stopped. He is on his knees and has begun to sing one of those folksongs that have followed us from Sherbrooke to Newfoundland across Canada and aboard the *Awatea*. I can feel my legs giving out and the bamboo pole cutting into my shoulders. The fog is breaking up and sunlight reflects off the sword as it falls, repeatedly, on his neck. He's remained somehow on his knees and has to be pushed over. One of them kicks Delisle's head down the small embankment into the sea.

Several of us are detailed to dig a shallow grave and he is buried, headless, beneath the runway of the Kai Tak airport.

Donnelly

The real heroes of Hong Kong
were the cooks and comedians.

When we returned
half of us were impotent.
One vet committed suicide
two weeks after his marriage.
Porteous took 3000 milligrams
of niacin daily until he died.

All we ever talked about was food.
— Howard, did I ever tell you
about my mother's pecan pies?
— No, Jack, I don't think you ever did.
Of course it was the hundredth time.
After the war, Jack sent me
a bushel of pecans from Texas.

We kept recipe books
instead of girlie magazines.
We'd have traded *Playboy*
for *Betty Crocker*
any day.

Berrigan

I'd been a teacher outside Yorkton,
so they put me in charge of the library.
There wasn't much variety,
some guys had read the same books
a dozen times. After a while,
they began to notice the words.
Four titles come to mind
as having more than literary signficance
for our situation. One was Maugham's
Of Human Bondage, a sort of case-book
for the physically and mentally lame POW.
Then there was *Down the Garden Path*.
Someone had crossed out the author's name
and written in "Mackenzie King."
Cheating Death was certainly popular,
but nothing had so much appeal
as Seton's *Wild Animals I Have Known*.
The text was surrounded with marginalia,
every blank space crammed with expletives
and commentary. Like biblical exegesis.
Seton was a Canadian and his stories
seemed to transport our captive audience
back home, even the stories set
in Nebraska or New Mexico.
I knew *Billy the Dog That Made Good*
and *Cute Coyote and Other Stories*
from my courses at teachers' college
in Saskatoon, but the all-time favourite
was "Lobo, King of Currumpaw," which
describes the capture and death of a wolf
after the killing of his mate, Blanca.
In the margin was scribbled: "Bullshit,
animals can't die of a broken heart."
Beneath that, in very precise script:
"Don't be too sure, mate. Signed,
a fellow-animal." I often wondered
about Seton's association

with the Boy Scouts of America.
He accused them of being militaristic,
so they threw him out in 1915,
ostensibly for not being an American.

Twelve

From the offices of the *South China Morning Post*, I could
watch the shipping in the harbour. Freighters of every size
and registry lay at anchor, waiting to unload raw materials
and pick up manufactured goods, much of it produced aboard
the flotilla of junks that scooted like water-beetles across the
skin of the bay. On the nearest of these junks, I could make
out children going about their tasks. They were unschooled
but sea-wise, tending animals and small shipboard gardens,
running errands and, when they were not babysitting, help-
ing at the sewing machines and assembling gadgets or toys
for foreign kids who'd never dirtied their hands with any-
thing but play. Floating operas that never stopped, despite the
rotations of the earth and the invention of the calendar.

Still, there was a freedom of sorts. These descendants of
traders and pirates, scorned and criticized for their unsavoury
aspect and links with crime, were the secret envy of many un-
derpaid and unprotected workers, who slept in shifts in the
densely populated slum-rises. They had helped Proulx escape
and now many of them were running illegals from Vietnam,
Cambodia, and the Mainland. For all I know, the junk I could
see refusing to give way to the Star Ferry and sending it off course
might be harbouring some precious human cargo, stowed away
amongst barrels of fuel oil and bales of cotton.

I'd have to wind things up soon. I had responsibilities to
assume back home in Edmonton. I'd left a note on my office
door that said simply: GONE FISHING, IN HONG KONG. A
lot of weight hung on that comma. And there was the mat-
ter of some articles I'd threatened to write for a friend at *The
Journal*: Britain's expiring lease on Hong Kong; the current
state of refugee camps; the night life and the black market.

"Why go to Hong Kong? You can get all the information you need from the computer data bank and imagine the rest."

We were sitting in the revolving restaurant of the Chateau Lacombe, across from his offices, while Edmonton disappeared under its annual snowfall. Two cars could not make the grade and were wedged, cross-wise, on the road below. Everything was grinding to a halt. Me, too.

"I've got to get out of here. You're probably right about the book, but there are things I have to find out. Facts, you know, impressions. I've been writing journalism for so long, I've forgotten how to invent."

The waitress brought the refills we'd ordered and a bill. My friend was a regular, but never had more than two drinks, which he referred to as his lube job. In a high-powered business that produced as much stress as information, he was a bastion of health and good sense. He'd been a good eighth man, a key, on the rugby team too. He was turning the drink in his hands and watching the amber liquid and ice gather momentum. When he stopped the glass, its contents continued their circuit of the container.

The junk had passed out of sight now, behind a high-rise under construction, one of those thirty-five-storey human beehives that were replacing the fifteen-storey variety. Construction workers moved soundlessly on bare feet along the narrow planks and bamboo scaffolding, secured only with hemp.

Bakaluk

You could hear the rumble of the bomb
70 miles away.

The Americans dropped
bras and panties
— then food.
First things first.

One relief container crashed through a hut
killing a POW.

On the way back home
I saw two movies in the canteen:
Donald Duck and *Frankenstein*.

The ship was called
the USS *Glory*.

from NO EASY EXIT (1989)

Little Windows

It's difficult now to speak of these things.
I'd rather describe the way light falls
in morning courtyards, on clothes
hung out to dry.
That child in the doorway
turning to the sound of the shutter,
half-smiling, half-indignant.
And Carmen's hair
filling the entire back window
of the Peugeot.

Fifteen square windows in the Lonquen
poster, a face in all but one.
Campesinos from Isla de Maipo
tortured and buried alive
in lime. Father
and three sons.
Windows of agent
Valenzuela's testimony:
a number killed at the air base,
others thrown into the sea
from helicopters, stomachs opened.

Each poster a small apartment building,
tenants gazing into the street
at some event, a demonstration,
a sunset. Eight more in Valparaiso
who should have looked out on the sea.

I saw bougainvillea
in a restaurant window
near the place of ambush;
and a window with a spiky cactus

in full bloom, a pottery pig
and a string of wicker birds
turning gently in the wind.

Why do they smile, these framed faces,
do they know something we don't?
Behind them perpetual white,
bright light
at the tunnel's end.
Perhaps it is we who are lost
and they looking out at us
from some perfect world,
wondering what all the fuss
is about, why
these masks of suffering.

When they break her eyes
images remain.
Sound of the helicopter
recedes. Sea is a window
above him, water
tongues the red from his stomach.

Human Rights Commission

The small woman seated before you describes her encoun-
ters with the military. In advance of the translation you hear
the phrase "caravan of death." She is not talking about a cir-
cus, her husband has not run away to a circus, though there
was one in town the day you arrived, the real McCoy. Me-
dieval etchings of the Dance of Death flicker in a dark recess
of your brain.

   Do you really want to hear this? Yesterday you were curi-
ous, took notes copiously. Numbers, implements of torture,
the general who travelled the provinces with his extermin-
ators and a chihuahua that sat on the back of the car seat
licking his ear.

October 23, 1973, the end of so much. Five months later she too is arrested, kept naked twenty days, a sack over her head. Kicks, blows, electricity, threats against the children, pretence her husband is still alive. You look again at this woman and wonder how much she is not telling you. A heated pipe. Rats driven into the vagina through a heated pipe.

When the interview began, the portable radio was playing "Moon Shadow" by Cat Stevens. A poster on the wall said, in Spanish: "No one disappears into thin air."

May Day

Part One

Okay, no story. Cariola Theatre, first of May,
streets empty except for the green armoured vans
affectionately known as butcher shops. Troops
at the ready, in their best Sunday riot gear.

Inside, singing *Adios, General,* I can hear
the rock band (half-rhyme with *carnaval*). Oops,
no story. Bass notes massage bone marrow. Any chance
soldiers prefer free verse? I admire the way

they're all on the job. Chicago mentioned, a riot
a hundred years ago, workers killed. The USA,
how Chileans love it still, the idea. Adrenalin,

body busy shucking its annual payload of dead skin,
sweat glands working overtime, how the letter "A"
dominates. Hand on the union card, eye on the exit.

Part Two

Grey canvas worker's gloves mounted
on a slab of wood absorb light
from slitted windows of the Vicaria.

A grim relic of those for whom Christ,
mounted also on wood, died. Performance
done, burden lifted, he stepped offstage

into the wings of his father's private staff
of angels. Each day priests pass
and families of the disappeared, eyes averted,
minds intent on the larger struggle.

They don't see axe, cart, or broom handle
and a thousand other implements of labour
radiating outwards, though part of them recalls
the words SOMOS MAS printed underneath.

Part Three

Yes, numbers count. Together we are more,
a force to be contended with, dumb cattle
driven into stadiums, broken, crushed like ore.
Watch us breed under the earth, battle

forces of darkness, our pit lamps
aglow. Third eyes. Coppery sweat
of our limbs. The general laughs,
but doesn't sleep well: new guards, SWAT,

screened applications. He suspects eucalyptus
of plotting against him. *Casi lo matan*, words
the leaves whisper: headlights bearing down,

screech of tires, gunfire from roadside bushes.
It adds up. Thanksgiving, revenge, woods
alive with birdsong, land no one can own.

Arpilleras

A woman cuts a triangle of corduroy
for a mountain, adjusts the cloth
so it rubs shoulders with another mountain,

candy-striped, and one cut from the sleeve
of a blue school tunic. Behind them
is a second range, probably

near the border in Argentina.
No one asks why distant mountains
are more exotic, with floral designs

from bright curtains, and catch more light,
not the school girls who stand with arms raised
in protest of the municipal order

closing their school, not the old-timers
leaning into death with their white wool hair
and matchstick canes. Her fingers tremble

as she cuts four houses from her husband's
best pair of trousers, worn once
to a christening, once to a union meeting,

and red canvas roofs from the raincoat of a daughter
who left suddenly at night by boat from Valparaiso.
She cross-stitches them to the sackcloth backing

to keep them in place, though she knows
nothing is secure against the night, the rumoured
fires. Tomorrow she will sell

her sackcloth tapestries for milk and beans
to feed the other children, but first
she must dream inhabitants in three dimensions,

the awkward, enduring women, moving
among the plaid windows and paisley shrubbery,
variously dressed, cut from the same cloth.

Supernova

We live by the grace
of past ages, old light
pulsing through millennia.

A cell divides,
a blue star, overhead, implodes
and burns gloriously
without thought.

Flowers get on with their business.

The man on the beach
does not notice, old heat
raising his expectations.
And the executive secretary
tanning her extravagant neck
among the dwarf trees
and city benches
has other worries:
angle of the tinfoil
reflector, the meaning
of loyalty, and finances,
always finances.
She wants sex most
when the emotional climate
makes it least likely.

Each earthly object
in its own turn
burns.

The little dictator,
who has made a coffin
of the ballot box
and fouled the riverbed
of dreams,
recalls the slogans
and Madison Avenue posters
that brought him power.

Old fears.

Everything tastes
of oblivion.

General Cemetery

Between the wrought-iron crosses of the disappeared
are no bored lions, avenues of eucalyptus;
here none go down to corruption

in the splendid isolation of crypt or mausoleum,
where empty skulls imagine their importance
and bones are wont to speak of privilege.

Between the wrought-iron crosses of the disappeared
you'll find no tributes to the intellect,
no verse inscriptions, no trace of Greece or Egypt

in the architecture. Add up the ragged columns
of the dispossessed and let archival winds
record each article of faith.

Between the wrought-iron crosses of the disappeared
only a half-starved dog can pass,
or a hummingbird, his heart in his throat.

He hovers overlong above the opened grave,
bearing witness to travesties
that do not stop with death in Santiago.

A woman's square-heeled shoe protrudes
from heaps of brick and bone, a patch of colour
showing through the skein of dust.

Between the wrought-iron crosses of the disappeared
her plastic heels are platforms of dissent;
her wit and candour, crimes against the state.

Place your flower gently now among the nameless dead
and let its beauty fade, its cut throat bleed,
into the silent, unassuming earth.

Decimas

Carabinero boulevards
in Bellavista, from downtown
to poorest barrios (rundown,
forgotten, God's precious discards).
From armoured trucks the junta guards
dispense their sinister blessings
liberally. We're confessing
to everything: slogans, joy,
love, left-wing thought, fire, scars, the boy
with Carmen Quintana, dressings.

Violetta Parra's clipped lines
will do quite nicely, thank you,
the strict form, repetitions too,
syntactical muscle, no spines
bent in submission. Work refines.
Neruda knew this; so did Yeats.
Power, in general, decimates.
Ten lines, eight syllables in each;

it takes no more than this to reach
the naked heart. Come, now, who waits?

This is not a country, he said,
only the draft of a country.
We are all revising, wintry
in our cages, our best dreams wed
to disaster, our best friends dead.
What to do, short of repentance?
Clean the barrel of each sentence,
keep dry the magazine of words.
Be nimble as dancers, goatherds,
dismantling the barbed-wire fence.

from GIRL BY THE WATER (1994)

Subsidies

A boy with a mechanical arm
addresses a group of kids
on farm safety;
a farmer tries to talk
to the camera — still asking himself
how it happened — youngest son, beside him
one moment on the fender,
slipping under the rear wheel of the tractor.

Eighty percent of rural deaths,
the voice explains,
are the result of farm accidents.

Statistics are no consolation
when you've seen the support-block
give way and the circular saw
walk through the flesh of your son's neck.
At night as you drift towards sleep
you see the recognition
in his startled eyes;
cock's crow
is the engine's whine.

A year later, you still can't look at her
over breakfast, rise
to the need in her flesh
or yours. You toy with an egg,
hard-boiled and intransigent
on your plate, invite
the coffee to burn your lips.

You hear them debate subsidies
in parliament, the future of the family farm,

and you know that nothing you plant
will ever again grow straight,
nothing you do
will ever make it right.

Junk Food Pastoral

Yours is the worst hay I cut,
Frank tells me, as he hoists another bale
onto the loaded wagon, where his wife
places it in interlocking fashion
over the previous layer, and the boy,
a late and unexpected child,
runs up and down the angled stooks.

I don't see Frank all winter, except to wave
as he drives home to family
and chores from the factory in Ottawa.
He speaks wistfully of retirement,
wondering how much steam he'll still have
when the nine-year-old leaves home.

A low yield this year, nine hundred bales,
fields overrun with straw weed,
hay I first charged him for, then shared,
and am now pleased just to have cut
to keep the thistles and burdock in check.

As the haywagon fills, he uses
the front-end loader with a sheet of plywood
to hoist six bales at a time.
This is their holiday, racing the weather,
ten loads in the heat of the day,
binder twine burning capable hands.

Rhythm of work. Smiles that take root
in stomach wall or rib-cage — they don't fade

easily. *Yours is the worst hay,* Frank is standing
eight feet above me on his plywood stage,
scenery of fast-moving cloud, *but my cows
seem to like it best.*

Weeping Tiles

The truck from the Moose Creek Septic Company
backs up under the maples and drops
its suctioning hose into the tank of brown sludge
recently unearthed. Fifteen years of domestic soup
percolating, all winter, below the frost line,
the incremental solids gathering volume
while the liquids disperse themselves
along a network of arteries under the lawn,
a cocktail for the fine hairs that line
the fingers of foraging root.

The driver, enormous hoe in hand,
stirs the broth, untroubled by the ripe legend
colouring the afternoon; he squats and balances
on the concrete lip of the sarcophagus
with the expectant air of a fisherman, or the boy
whose straw will soon vanquish a milkshake.
For him there's no rich archive to discover,
no reservoir of dreams or deep images —
sediment not sentiment, an antiquated holding tank
and a violated bed of weeping tiles.

The Sporting Life

What training, what twisted circuitry,
enables him to kill a woman
with a high-powered rifle

and head into the hills, moving easily
across packed snow, leaving little scent
and no tracks?

Snowmobile in driveway, ridge
of low hills overlooking Crag Lake, two
stainless steel chimneys, a double swing-seat
hanging in the porch, and across the photo
a broad plastic band bearing the warning:
Police Line Do Not Cross. In French:
Passage Interdit.

The manuals describe an independent woman
as a threat to the abuser, whose wife stays
home out of fear. Big game guide
and taxidermist, he prefers his women
docile, stuffed, and easily mounted.
This stranger to the area, an engineer
for the City of Whitehorse, a land claims
negotiator who lived alone and was
capable of bucking wood, building
an addition to the cabin
at kilometre ten on Tagish Road
without the help of men,
crossed the line
into forbidden territory,
intervened. For this,
she encountered a claim that could not
be negotiated, blasted a hole
in all her arguments.

Reporters for *The Yukon News*
and *The Whitehorse Star*
adhere to the protocols of investigative journalism,
using only the word suspect,
though one speculates on the danger to people
working with battered women
from men who have nothing to lose.

Mother and two sons in protective custody,
community in shock,
the killer at large with his anger, blond
moustache, list of names, and
possibly blue eyes.

Meanwhile, the emergency response team,
the pilot, the police dog
and handler have begun the hunt,
men trained in the use of weapons, survival
in subarctic temperatures, who know
penetration precedes the sound
of gunfire. Layers of skin,
futile as plastic barriers.

At the Downtown Hotel

Allen's an asshole. I knew that all along,
but still I stuck it out. Stupid, eh?
That's Alice. I can feel the spit
from the word *stupid* strike my cheek
as she reaches for a second beer.

The three women seated with me
are genuine sourdoughs: a nurse,
a civil servant, and ardent Alice,
threatening to become gainfully employed
now she's dumped Allen.
We're the only patrons. The others
are sweating it out with an amateur band
waging war on silence at the Eldorado.

I tell them Peter's story about recommending
further education to a youth who quit school
to work as a miner. The kid
pointed to Peter's dilapidated pickup and said:

Why, for that? I worked two summers
and I've already got a brand new GMC.

A rumour is going the rounds that a company
will put down a hardrock mine nearby
and bring in five hundred families,
but not to Dawson itself. Peter offered it
as fact, but Buffalo, who manages the airstrip
and only taxi in town, sounded skeptical.

I'm trying to figure out what keeps the town alive,
other than tourism and National Historic Sites,
but Alice hasn't finished with Allen yet, though
she's demolished both beers. The three women
are nodding and laughing. Then Pat says:
Ya, he was an asshole even ten years ago
when he was married to me.

Afterbirth

for Irene (Turner) Geddes, 1913-1947

Absence: the way the lost tooth drives the curious tongue
and alters, utterly, the architecture of the mouth.

First, there was nothing; then these relics appeared
in brown wrapping paper, with string
and requisite postage —

> *cameo pendant with antique scrolled filigree*
> *and a woman's face carved in profile;*

> *a serving plate,*
> *Royal Staffordshire porcelain,*
> *Cairo pattern, riot*
> *of hand-painted flowers*
> *on thick blue stems,*

central ring of geometric swirls
that resemble an Arab carpet
and, not exactly random,
fifteen peacock eyes
ringed in gold
and blue

fragments of your life arriving in the mail
after forty years, not exactly
posthaste.

❋

Ragged paintings fallen from the door of the refrigerator,
flush of cheek bending to lace my shoe.

Even your best friend Ann, married to a fireman,
was helpless when the wind shifted
and the burn went deep. So disturbed
she didn't take me to the funeral.

I entered the water at English Bay
and wandered too far along the crowded beach.
A policeman brought me back
from Main and Hastings, bathing suit
still wet, face smeared with Neapolitan ice cream.

Things I can't discard — fire and water, the blight
of the seemingly extraneous.

❋

Ann, who claimed the plate was seldom bereft
of cookies, also included

two plastic cigarette cases:
one for the coffee table,
transparent with yellow lid;

the other, wine-dark and narrow,
with sliding lid, for a purse
or pocket, each bearing
the name Renee, or Irene.

I recall Jim Friesen, his cold Mennonite name,
who cut owls and deer from plastic, the thin blade
of his jigsaw carving a delicate ear, how he
populated the basement flat in Kerrisdale
with his transparent creatures, keeping death at bay
and taming the fierce sheet metal hopper
of the furnace, an inverted pyramid
of sawdust.

✳

I was eating gingersnaps and nursing a beer
the evening of the CBC documentary
on prenatal growth. Last
of the night-owls. There on the screen,
composed in its grid of amniotic dots,
the human ear, like the wings of Mercury,
seemed to sprout from a heel and work its way
to thigh and head, gathering as it went
its water music, coral
symphonies.

Womb, the place
of generation.

Cells multiply, run to excess. Cobalt
turns the tumour
into ash.
Would it were so.
Garden verses, my song rooting
in walls of soft flesh.

✳

Family legend has you playing piano
and singing "September Song"
or swimming the distance
from Fisherman's Cove to Point Atkinson,
just off the starboard quarter
of the boat. Days spent at Eaton's
as a demonstrator — lipstick, white uniform, sundry
foodstuffs. Then the contest at Orpheum Theatre:

MISS WRIGLEY'S SPEARMINT GUM

＊

Mother is a dairy cow,
her breasts are made of silk.
Her life is an emporium,
her death a crematorium;
I love the taste of ashes in my milk.

Non omnis moriar.

Disassembled (or is it dissembled?) pieces,
something for the Orphic sailor boy
to chew on.

＊

No Grecian urn or enamelled vase,
only (I apologize for having to record it),

> *a slender tea-canister*
> *of cheap tin*
> *and made in China.*
> *Four of the eight panels*
> *sport dragons.*
> *A figure in purple robes*
> *and Fu Manchu beard*
> *reclines on a couch,*
> *served by women*

or solicited to buy silk;
I can't tell which.
Runners of a small sled
perhaps intended to haul
a wine-jug,
intrude into the scene.
Next door, the wise man
holds up a rock or fortune cookie
for an admirer to see,
or a disciple.
Behind the red fence
what's left of a stylized landscape:
rocks and trees, scrolls
of cloud, pine cones
the shape of hairbrushes.

Details worn away, a convex lid that measures leaves
no one can read.

❀

I squeezed the last drop of colour from the beleaguered
tea-bag and set about opening the bundle from Ann,
which contained an eight-page letter. Shards,
things learned underfoot or by osmosis
in the womb, potent
waters steaming with plankton.

Years ago, in the room on First Avenue,
the visiting poet, holding court on a blue futon,
listened to my mother-stories,
rubbed the basset's belly with her stockinged foot
until it ejaculated on the rug,
then said: You speak with affection
to cover up your anger.

❀

Wine-dark, how the discourse
betrays us. And *bereft*, the dynamic
of transference; my own emptiness
assigned to a cookie-plate.

You at fourteen, stretched out full length
on the Star's running board, or
younger still, photographed on the lawn
with different animals, your ringlets
perfectly framing the head
of the bulldog. So much of Vancouver
still bush, couch grass. Propped on an elbow
in the sand, pleated skirt
the scallop on the Shell Oil sign.

The migrating ear
never sleeps.

❀

Drop the spoon, the mother disappears;
undo each lace, she ties it up again.

The Chinese have a phrase, *yü shih*, which translates,
roughly, as leftover history. If it's not
available, invent it.

Hours spent with Ann, shared laughter, room
for the outrageous, what is natural but otherwise
designated crude. My small face at your breast
and the husband,
           remote,
                    dreaming a freedom
of uniforms, regimentation, perhaps
death, and how to forgive him
that, ever.

❀

Blue-veined placenta, my garment-shroud, buried
beneath the rosebush in Kerrisdale. Assume,
again, this mantle of earth. Plaything,
mother-child, Scheherezade, rehearsing
your unforgettable cameo
in a pocket.

When the nightmares stopped
and your sad, concerned face
disappeared from the second-floor
landing, I felt the song
rise in my throat,
deep, plaintive, voice
of the lost tribes
of Israel, waters of the Red Sea
drawing back to engulf
Pharoah's armies,
and the cry
of those perishing
in the black and white stage-sets
of MGM.

        Cairo,
the pattern more than serves
its purpose. Things
of beauty, things of no
account. Against such odds,
locating the words,
the mother-

lode.

Cod Royal

You take your place at the piano,
adjust the chair, and lean
into the music. Your thin wrists poised
above the keyboard are the stately
necks of swans. I loved best
your earliest performance — how you sang
when the first wave of oxygen
broke across your scalp, flooded the lung cavities,
and drowned you into cadence.

So engine's hum is the amniotic
tide and the ticking clock
a surrogate heart.

❋

Each syllable a breast to drain, each word
an island asking to explore.

Lumblums, you said, as the sirens grew faint
in the rain-soaked night. Of those,
you were well informed, camping out in an oxygen tent
at the Edmonton General when the fevers
wouldn't break and tepid baths
brought no relief.

After twelve months of faulty diagnoses
left us slumped over catalogued
symptoms in medical dictionaries,
your tonsils and adenoids floated into history
down the storm drains to the North Saskatchewan.

You clung to me in the doorway of the operating room,
blood from the haemorrhaging stitches
bright at the corners of your mouth, and said,

> *It's all right, Dod,*
> *don't cry.*

＊

Though Ecclesiastes never mentioned it,
there is a time for vitamins,
the horrible D variety that backs up the drain
and makes your mouth the floor
of a gutting shed.

You place your lips around the rubbery pill
and the effort to swallow
makes your small body shudder.

＊

I never knew you'd broken your collarbone
until you said, climbing stairs with me
from the basement,

>   *Take my good hand, Dad.*

For years I'd sit at the foot of your bed late at night
and listen to you breathe, inhale the newness.

Then you were in school and practising piano,
your chubby fingers nowhere near the keys
for "Traffic Cop," "Swans on the Lake."

＊

Each year I mark your new height
in pencil in the entrance
to the laundry room
or count feet
and syllables in the dream
that is summer, my heart
crying,
>   *adagio, adagio,*

your legs pumping, hair
thrown back, a brush stroke of light
against the green of lawn, of
maples, higher and higher,
the relentless swing
a pendulum

or metronome.

✯

On your feet again, bowing, face obscured
beneath a canopy of hair.

My heart goes out, gives back the words
you shaped when the hours were
long, the pill bitter.

You placed your red stool beside the kitchen table
and reached for the bottle of cod liver oil pills.
When I inquired of your intentions,
you lifted the plastic lid of the garbage container
under the sink and said, with the authority
of a policeman,
>   *No more cod royal.*

✯

If, on the stage you inherit, encores
are still allowed, I leave this poem as record
of my request. Know, too, that somewhere

in the audience a drowned sailor, his swamped
heart rocking in its cage of bone,
sings your praise without intermission,
lungs emptied of all utterance.

Girl by the Water

1. Artist

Only the girl by the water attracts me.
Soldiers, with pomp and pretension, parading colours
in the distant square, mean nothing.

Hair ochre, not auburn; head tilted a little forward, nape
bare to wind or axe or lover's mouth.
The quiet ache her beauty causes reverberates
back along the taut thread of my being to its obscure
and infinitesimal beginnings.

Yes, yes, you say, fanciful talk,
a doddering antiquity
passing off each urge (or demi-urge) as aesthetics.
Skip the rhetoric; give us the old
blind thrust in the dark.
Humour the artist; you'll not find
Eros lacking in the oils.

She peers intently at something in her palm, perhaps
a map of the future. Will there be children?
Will one come to grief, and how
to endure that? Amused
by reminders, in a congruence of lines,
but not foolish enough
to think these qualities a guarantee.

Without lowering her hand, she looks
across the water and locates
the wavering V of departing geese. Though young,
she is no stranger to loss; the sounds
these travellers make recall her to a simple errand
not yet completed. She gathers her skirts
and begins to run towards the square, the milling soldiers,
where, lamb to slaughterer's blade, she surrenders
her heart for the hint of a smile.

2. Chambermaid

She had clogs in one hand, money in the other.
I was there on the pier, close enough
to see her count the coins
and drop them in an apron pocket.

We worked together mornings
at the inn, five till noon.
A dozen reeking chamber-pots,
wood, ironing, beds to make;
it took us hours to scrub the smell of piss
and ashes from our hands.

The man in question was not old.
Whatever business brought him into town
would not detain him long.
I'd guess the coach was hired;
the horses, though freshly groomed,
were unnaturally lean
and one, a gelding, would not stop
chewing on the bit.

I thought she shuddered
once or twice
before she turned to leave.
I'm still amazed to think
her feet were bare.

3. Priest

She had something to confess.
I was half-asleep
and did not catch the details.

To tell the truth, I was having trouble
concentrating on the petty sins
of parishioners, when I had my own lusts

to contend with. Gluttony, choirboys,
Christ's blood by the gallon.

She spoke of voices.
This was new in one so young.

Her breasts were exquisitely formed,
though tightly bound;
and I could faintly distinguish
something on her wrist
when she made the sign of the cross.
It might have been a birthmark
or a bruise. *Mea culpa.*

I erred, so be it;
I didn't want to miss the arrival
of the boats with their catch
of fresh cod. A thousand
Hail Marys every four hours,
before meals. Later,
when I saw her at the shore
listening to her voices,
I couldn't shake
this tag of schoolboy Latin:

*Menses, menses,
the Lord's amanuensis.*

4. Aunt

Who could blame her for those hours by the river,
where it bellies out and wind catches the sails
of sea-going vessels. She was wearing the vest
with the velvet smocking usually reserved for Sundays,
which I'd given her after my fourth child.
God knows, it would never fit me
again. She spent an afternoon in the window seat
making alterations, cocooned in her thoughts

and a low, tuneless humming. Outside, cobbles
glistened and gave off steam after the sudden
shower; I looked up from my bowl of batter
in time to see two horses rear in their traces
and the coach clatter to an agitated stop. I screamed
and ran to the door to look for my youngest,
leaving doughy prints on the wood and handle.

He'd heard nothing and remained transfixed
by his make-believe saucepan boat and the puddle
that contained it. She stood in the doorway
as the coach rounded the corner, the velvet smocking
aglow in gathered light, and looked at the bright
bead of blood on her thumb. *You frightened me*,
she said, wiping the injured area clean on her tongue.

She seemed young, I forgave her
the trust she still harboured, the hope,
and for artlessly animating my loutish husband.

5. *Private*

They questioned me, of course. Soldiers
are fair game: bastions of good deeds
in battle, but animals in town.
The spoils of war. My own sister
raped, but not by soldiers.

I saw her crouched in an empty stall
in the barn, watching the blood and sperm
drip between her fingers. Years later,
I helped my father die slowly.

My wagon pinned him to the wall
of the granary, while the team
of Belgians, deaf to his cries, danced
on the spot. I was drunk

when the girl entered a shop and the curtains
were drawn; for all I knew,
she was the owner's daughter.

6. Merchant

A few pennies, no more. There was great noise
and brouhaha in the square, enough
to interfere with my accounts.
A wave of sound swept inside
when the door opened. Otherwise, I might
not have noticed her, bent
over goods and produce at the counter.

Three soldiers lounged in the doorway, tongues
hanging out, and I had to draw the latch
to get rid of them. News of defeat carries fast
and this rough lot was next in line, vessels loading
all day at anchor, coal barges and small skiffs
strung out beside them in the slow current.

Think about it. A pity to go to your grave
ignorant of the other great mystery.
Still, I have no proof.

She toyed with a pear and an apple, then held
a remnant of white muslin to her cheek.
It didn't add up, the vacant look,
the way her fingers brushed the tops
of sundry items. She might have propositioned me
or purchased candies. Instead,
she placed her sweating pennies in the charity box
for the families of lost mariners.
More laughter, shouting. Door closed,
and a small quantity of sand
on the floor.

7. Lawyer

The only evidence we have that's overriding
is the fact she's disappeared. Guardians
asked us not to publish;
the governing council cautioned,
for the public good, to await news
from the front. My obligation's

to the law. I reconstruct the morning
from myriad clues, then retire
to my club to rinse the foul taste
from my mouth. At night I dream
my own complicity, the violence,
lies, the hot desire. The girl
I search for is six months younger
than the child who eats
at this table, calls me father.

How can I know what she thinks
of me any more than I know the limits
of my own depravity? The hand
she extends, will I cut it off at the wrist
and enter it as evidence?

What kind of advocate is this
who listens to the requiem of pain
and feels his own sex rise.

8. Midshipman

She had a small anchor,
not much larger than a wasp,
tattooed on her wrist before I left
on the first troop ship.

I was in the crow's nest
with a bosun's pipe

when we hoisted the aftersheets.
I could see her on the rocks
of the Eggerton Head promontory
waving, holding up her anchor,
and listening for the three short blasts
I'd promised to make.

I suppose we were lovers,
though without the usual
haste and burning.
I'd touched her naked breasts
and she was not ashamed
to admit her curiosity.
We talked, collected shells
at Eggerton Head, and thought
an earlobe worth an afternoon.

Drowning wasn't half so bad
and I carried that tiny anchor
with me to my grave.

9. Mother

Who are the real freaks
at the carnival?

Fathers, uncles, educators,
all obsessed with my hole,
prodding me with words, objects,
themselves. Step this way, gentlemen,
see the vortex, the grave,
the black rent
from which all things come
and into which it all disappears.

That's it, pretend you're shocked.

You couldn't even wait for breasts
to advertise my plum, my garden
plot, my anchorage, third
eye you must all investigate,
porthole into paradise
or hell. What could I say to her
as a mother that would be useful
without breaking her heart

or her will? I kept my distance
and my counsel, gave her up
for adoption, and used my earnings
to protect her. She never saw
through my disguise, the rented coach,
the childless couple with their books
and picnic baskets.

10. Herself

A strong easterly was blowing
off Eggerton Head, so surface driftwood
seemed stationary, despite the fast
current in the narrows. I folded
my clothes neatly in a crevice
above the high-water line and wrapped myself
loosely in white muslin, cutting armholes,
and drawing in the waist with pins
and ribbon. I'd let the merchant cheat me
in my purchases, knowing he was old enough
to be distracted by his greed.

My mother and her favourite customer
would not consent to leave me here
until I confided I'd meet my beau
within the hour. I never loved her more
than at that moment, for her madness
and extravagance. Voices told me

he was dead a week before the news
arrived in town. I made my peace
with God, blessed the aunt who taught me
how to sew, and kissed a drunken soldier
on the cheek before I quit the square.

The wind eased. I formed a whistle
with a blade of grass between my thumbs
and blew three times. Does every bride
have goosebumps? Driftwood moved
towards the sea; the water took me
in its strong embrace.

from THE PERFECT COLD WARRIOR *(1995)*

Nablus, October

i.

Too late for lemons and languor.
Beyond the walls idleness
skedaddles, eros
close at heels

An olive tree, blackened
by fire, glances over its shoulder
at the retreating azure
hills
      a tethered goat
ejaculates freely
on the confiscated dunams

ii.

At the town hall a man
in a wheelchair
recalls muscled legs
that carried him into surrounding
hills, impact of blast, the car
cantilevered between two
doorways

and a painting of the prophet,
invisible from crotch
down in the muddy waters
of the Jordan,
laughing while a disciple
douses him

iii.

Economies of scale

Sabbath leaves
bale out, imperial summer's
taken to its heels

a beer can glints in sunlight
by the checkpost

What Does A House Want?

A house has no unreasonable expectations
of travel or imperialist ambitions;
a house wants to stay
where it is

A house does not demonstrate
against partition or harbour
grievances;
        a house is a safe
haven, anchorage, place
of rest

Shut the door on excuses
— greed, political expediency

A house remembers
its original inhabitants, ventures
comparisons:
        the woman
tossing her hair
on a doorstep, the man
bent over his tools and patch
of garden

What does a house want?

Laughter, sounds
of love-making, to strengthen
the walls;
                    a house
wants people, a permit
to persevere

A house has no stones
to spare; no house has ever been convicted
of a felony, unless privacy
be considered a crime in the new
dispensation

What does a house want?

Firm joints, things on the level, water
rising in pipes

Put out the eyes, forbid
the drama of exits,
entrances; somewhere
in the rubble a mechanism
leaks time,
                    no place
familiar for a fly
to land
on

from *Norwegian Rabbit* (*The Trotsky Poems*)

12

Passionate? Yes, but lame and certainly
not wasp-waisted. By the time we met
she was spending whole days in a wheelchair
or in hot baths for relief. It's fair to say
I was taken with her wit, crude
humour, and almost primitive intelligence.

We were installed in the Blue House
in Coyoacan and spent too long in the role
of honoured guests for anyone to tolerate.
My work went on, regardless. In arguments
she often took my side, infuriating Diego,
especially after his long absences.
The intimacy she insinuated was designed
to make him jealous. I wasn't immune
to her game: flattering an old man with headaches
and high blood-pressure. Predictably,
I couldn't concentrate on writing
when she sat in the same room with a book.

The blow-up came when I tried to explain
the "neither war nor peace" strategy
that had guided our negotations
with the Kaiser's minions in Brest-Litovsk.
Diego was drinking heavily and Frida,
as conspicuously as possible, placed the bottle
of tequila just beyond his reach. Natalia Sedova
had abandoned diplomacy for bed,
but the door to our room was slightly ajar,
so I knew she was not sleeping. Diego
could not be convinced that the stalling tactics
had succeeded and kept pointing out
the harsher terms of the eventual peace agreement.

He was a good Communist, but pressure
from the Stalinist trade unions to sever connections
with me was building. It's perfectly obvious,
Frida announced, turning her chair dismissively
in my direction. He grabbed her cane
and pulled the tequila towards him with the crook,
drinking straight from the bottle. Frida's
smile froze him in that position for several seconds
before the bottle shattered on the table edge.

Several chairs overturned as he crashed
through the house to the street, cursing.
I realized later he was sober enough
to make a linguistic distinction between the verbs
stall and *delay*. Peace was delayed by fog,
he said, but Trotsky has stalled in this house
for two years. In the silence that followed,
I could hear the click of Natalia Sedova's door.

19

I was criticized for not fraternizing,
not putting in appearances at the ballet
or giving lavish parties for my friends
and associates. Socializing — is this
what it means to be a socialist?

Shrewd as I am said to be in terms
of theory, I lack a capacity
for intrigue. Ferocious in defence
of revolution, to quote Lenin,
yet I formed no alliances
to protect me against calumny,
careerists. Society bores me,
though individuals may be as curious
and engaging as books. Take
Cardenas, for example. No, not

el presidente, who granted me asylum;
I don't move in those circles
anymore. Frida Kahlo's gardener, who'd
lost a leg fighting for Zapata
near Veracruz, confessed quite openly
his faith in vegetables. Fallen
in one of the hacienda's cultivated
gardens, he'd made a tourniquet
from grape vines, then stuffed himself
with tomatoes and carrots before
passing out. *I've devoted my life*
to vegetables, not politics. Brown face
a nest of furrows, yet the smile
unmistakable beneath his hat brim.
Squinting into sunlight and using
the shovel handle for balance
as he rolls another cigarette.

Sometimes I listen to my own voice
on the wax recording surface
and have to laugh. I have no talent
for small talk, though I can hold forth
for hours on points of doctrine,
certain species of plant.

Don't get me started on cacti.

Cardenas' wooden leg, scrubbed
and drying by the adobe wall,
rises from its detachable
foot like an exclamation mark.
He takes the drink I offer,
raises an arm in mock salute:

¡Viva Patata!

Etymology

Sometimes during spelling bee
I get to wondering about the origin
of words. *Parenthetical*, for example,

what does it have to do with parents?
This leads to questions
about my own murky origins

and images of my father in rut.
I consider the women in his life: my mother
long since dead from reproductive

cancer, "that Bruner woman" who lives
near the construction site in Saltcoats
and was built into family legend

while my stepmother gave birth to her
first and only natural child.
Others? Most likely, given the way

his rude, inquisitive hands
violate the space of guests, female
relatives, as if the body

and its parts are public property.
A puritan when it comes to the sexual habits
of others, he can't bear to hear

a dirty joke spoken in mixed company,
complains of skimpy costumes, and even
near the end at eighty suspects himself

duped and cuckolded. I observe him,
fascinated, the man who made me,
genetic coding and all, bequeathed

his weak back and poorly evolved arthritic
feet, his fishy inheritance and love
of boats, all those ancestors

scuttling among rocks and Scottish
estuaries. But that's not why I classify
each gesture, cross-examine witnesses

who claim to know him. It's
the other I seek, the one whose hands
stray from gillnet and carpentry,

healing labour, the time-
bomb of the father I carry like a
ticking clock inside.

False Creek

My father keeps his gillnetter moored
over the winter at False Creek,
where a single mill remains and a few

local industries and trucking companies
occupy the shoreline and flatland
under the Granville Bridge. I ride my bike
down Terminal Avenue, past railyards

and shipping sheds, and leave it lying
on the wharf while I pump dry
the reeking bilge. The flats have their own

bouquet, especially at low tide, a nauseating
funk of primal ooze that spawns
species predestined
to replace us. Everything in the boat

is damp and sometimes the water level
rises over the floorboards in the cockpit,
where tin cans and other items float

and knock against the drum and ribs
as I bail furiously. My recurring
nightmare is to find the boat submerged,
only the mast protruding

from the black, oily water, pointing
its accusing finger at me. Minnows
and bottom feeders will swim

through the cabin, brushing the glass
of the wheelhouse with cold gill
and gossamer fin. The compass
gives no direction; the eight spokes

of the helm are a child's sun, passing
a night of wet, cold comfort
under the sea, in league with starfish

and other creatures of the deep. I try
to escape this dream on my bicycle
but water impedes my movements,
pedals turning in slow motion

and my heart pumping wildly
past the stalled cars and ghostly red traffic
light at Terminal and Main.

Damaged Goods

My father brings home merchandise
from the warehouse at Macintosh Cartage
that's smoke-damaged, parts

of a shipment of plaster wall hangings,
trios of airborne ducks that can fly
in any direction or formation,
depending which way and on which wall

you hang them. Black velvet paintings,
exotic feminine profiles, chocolates,
and imported tea-sets. A trailer-load

of goodies up for grabs, already written off
by the insurance company. Everyone
he knows in Grandview is on the alert,
making space for plaster drakes

and mallards, high-flyers all. There are
even dress shirts that did not escape
unscathed inside their plastic packaging.

How he loves it, my skid-road Rockefeller,
Santa of the smokehouse, not just delivering
the goods, but dispensing largesse, his heart
expanding to the task. Even now the paternal

corpse speaks out, scripting my narrative.
Where is this man I seek to credit
and to blame? He is here inside, alien

but perfectly at home in his self-created
host. Big-time spender, eating my heart out,
distributing my organs among friends, a great squid
squirting his black ink through my veins,

authoring destiny, continuance,
the ball-and-chain of my being. No exile,
no extradition order, can touch him;

he has survived war, prohibition, the myth
of origins. Each day I kill and resurrect him
as required. Thesis, antithesis, dialectic
of desire, denying inheritance, yet

potlatching its resources. Father and son,
and that third duck in the plaster trinity —
joker, trickster, monkey-king, wild card!

Active Trading

I come by my taste for disaster
naturally, raised in a district
bounded by Commercial Drive,
Broadway, and Terminal Avenue:

money, showbiz, death, the secular
trinity. Weekends and after school,
I watch wrecks jockeyed
around the sheet metal enclosure

at Clark and Hastings, the automobile
graveyard with its crushed Fords
and devastated Chevies occupying
common ground. Cranes,

meticulous, hoist an Edsel, casualty
of a species already endangered
on the drawing-board, to the privacy
of restoration shed, and a quaint

torpedo-nosed Studebaker, totalled
in a spectacular four-vehicle accident

on the Trans-Canada. Up close
telltale signs, brown stains

on the dash and upholstery, mute
predictable dolls with false eyelashes
and feigning sleep. Thus I evolve,
celebrant of the car-crash, and

contemplate the bruised colours
under lamplight. The wall
of reflecting hubcaps a constellation
of stars and minor planets; racks

of bumpers, grilles, Crusaders' armour.
The Perfect Cold Warrior, ready
for anything: earthquake, Armageddon,
Social Credit. The world my

gritty oyster: insurance, commodities,
even journalism. My pulsing
proboscis picks up advance signals
of the Second Narrows Bridge collapse

hours before my father, with diving suit
and acetylene torch, is recruited
to cut bodies from the Lego
of twisted girders. Language, my stock

in trade, provides clues: *landslide,
write-off, head-on, impending.*
I align myself with Cassandra,
Suzuki, McNeil-Lehrer, I.F. Stone.

I think everyone loves calamity.
I come running with the latest bad news
only to be rebuked and set upon
outside the city gates.

BOOKS by GARY GEDDES

POETRY
Poems, 1971
Rivers Inlet, 1972
Snakeroot, 1973
Letter of the Master of Horse (1970), 1973
War and Other Measures, 1976
The Acid Test, 1980
The Terracotta Army, 1984
Changes of State, 1986
Hong Kong, 1987
Selected Writings of Gary Geddes, translated into Chinese
by Peng Jia-lin, 1988
No Easy Exit / Salida difícil, 1989
Light of Burning Towers: Poems New and Selected, 1990
Girl by the Water, 1994
The Perfect Cold Warrior, 1995

FICTION
The Unsettling of the West, 1986

NON-FICTION
Letters from Managua: Meditations on Politics and Art, 1990

DRAMA
Les Maudits Anglais, 1984

TRANSLATION
I Didn't Notice the Mountain Growing Dark (with George Liang),
poems of Li Pai and Tu Fu, 1986

CRITICISM
Conrad's Later Novels, 1980

ANTHOLOGIES
20th-Century Poetry and Poetics, 1969, 1973, 1985, 1996
15 Canadian Poets Times 2, 1971, 1977, 1988
Skookum Wawa: Writings of the Canadian Northwest, 1975
Divided We Stand, 1977
The Inner Ear, 1983
Chinada: Memoirs of the Gang of Seven, 1983
Vancouver: Soul of a City, 1986
Compañeros: Writings about Latin America (with Hugh Hazelton), 1990
The Art of Short Fiction: An International Anthology, 1993

ACKNOWLEDGEMENTS

I would like to thank the editors of the various magazines, newspapers, and anthologies in which some of these poems have appeared, including *The Observer*, *The Globe and Mail*, *The Edmonton Journal*, *Ambit*, *Poetry Australia*, *The Malahat Review*, *Queen's Quarterly*, *CV/II*, *Fiddlehead*, *The Honest Ulsterman*, *Tribune*, *Rhinoceros*, *The Dublin Review*, *The Penguin Book of Canadian Verse*, *Tuatara*, *Saturday Night*, *Border Crossings*, *Storm Warning*, *Under Another Sky*, *The Republic of Conscience*, *The Moosehead Review*, *Playing with Fire*, *Prism International*, *Island*, *Tamarack Review*, and *Hong Kong Literature*. Thanks to Per Brask, of the Theatre Department at the University of Winnipeg; to CBC Radio; and to BBC Third Programme. I am grateful to my previous publishers, Talonbooks, Oberon, Coteau, Turnstone, Anansi and Véhicule, for permission, where still necessary, to reprint. I am grateful to the Canada Council, the Ontario Arts Council, the Bureau of International Cultural Relations of the Department of Foreign Affairs, and Concordia University for financial support during the research for and writing of these poems.